T0283483

Mac & Cheese Adventure

A World of Cheesy Delights!

Table Of Contents

Introduction

Welcome Young Chefs! Get ready to embark on a cheesy and delightful journey that's all about a global twist on everyone's favorite comfort food - Mac & Cheese!

Macaroni and cheese has a fascinating story, believed to have originated in Europe before making its way across the Atlantic. It was in America that it truly found its fame, transforming from an elite delicacy to a household staple. This recipe book is a celebration of its evolution and diversity, a guide to experimenting with new flavors, and an invitation to create joyful family memories around the kitchen table.

Inside this book, you'll find 25 amazing Mac & Cheese recipes inspired from around the world. Each recipe is designed to be a culinary adventure that you and your family can embark on together. From classic comfort to exotic explorations, there's something here for everyone, no matter your taste buds' passport stamps.

Have fun and enjoy your cooking journey. Making Mac & Cheese is an adventure —a wonderul chance to bond with loved ones, share stories, and create something special together.

So, buckle up..it's time to dive into the cheesy world of Mac & Cheese and explore flavors from around the globe.

Let's fire up those stovetops, toss some pasta, and create delicious dishes and memories that will last a lifetime. **Let's Go Chefs!**

About Chef KC

@ LetsGoChefKC

Hi there! I'm Kristina, but you can call me Chef KC.

I'm not just a chef; I'm a mother who's been passionate about cooking since I was a young chef myself. I find immense joy in sharing fun recipes and showing young chefs all the incredible tricks of the culinary trade. My children, family, and friends from all around the world have been the inspiration for my recipes. A collection of favorites that I am sharing for everyone to enjoy.

Now, let me spill the tea on one of my specialties—baked goods. You see, there's something truly magical about the way flour, sugar, butter, and a dash of love can transform into delectable treats that make hearts and taste buds dance with delight.

But here's the icing on the cake (pun intended): My recipes have graced the menu at the prestigious Royale Tea Room in La Jolla, California. Can you imagine sipping tea and indulging in small bites and treats baked with love...all while enjoying the ocean breeze? It's a dream come true and I'm here to sprinkle a little bit of that magic into your own kitchen.

Stay tuned for more scrumptious recipes, handy kitchen tips, and a whole lot of culinary fun from Chef KC. Your taste buds are in for a treat!

Coming Soon:

The Cheese Book for Young Chefs
The Royale Tea Room - Small Bites and Pastries
Mac & Cheese Adventure - Volume 2

Safety First

Cooking is super fun, but it's important to remember that safety always comes first.

Here are some essential tips to ensure you stay safe while whipping up delicious dishes in the kitchen:

1. **Get an Adult's Permission:** Always ask a parent or guardian for permission before you start cooking. They can help you gather ingredients, use appliances, and guide you when needed.

2. **Wash Those Hands**: Before you touch any food, make sure you wash your hands with soap and warm water for at least 20 seconds. Clean hands keep your food safe from germs!

3. **Stay Organized:** Gather all your ingredients and utensils before you begin. This way, you won't have to rush around the kitchen looking for things while the stove is on.

4. **Knife Safety:**If you're using a knife, be super careful! Ask an adult to show you the right way to hold it and how to cut ingredients safely. Always cut away from your fingers.

5. **Heat Awareness:** The stove and oven can get really hot. Make sure to use oven mitts or potholders when handling hot pans, pots, or baking sheets. Don't forget to turn off the stove when you're done!

6. **Mindful Mixing:** When you're stirring hot liquids or sauces, make sure the pot or pan is stable on the stove. Hold the handle and stir slowly to avoid spills.

7. **Fire Safety:** Know where the fire extinguisher is in your kitchen, just in case. And never, ever throw water on a grease fire. Instead, use a lid to smother the flames or an adult can use the fire extinguisher.

8. **Ask for Help:** If you ever feel unsure about something or if you accidentally cut yourself or get burned, don't hesitate to ask a grown-up for help. They're there to keep you safe!

9. **Tasting Tips:** It's okay to taste your food, but use a clean spoon each time and never lick your fingers while you're cooking. This helps prevent germs from getting into your dishes.

10. **Clean Up:** After your delicious meal is ready, it's time to clean up. Ask for help with washing dishes, and make sure all appliances are turned off.

Safety First

Parents are like kitchen superheroes, and they're always ready to assist when needed. Here are some situations when it's best to call them for backup:

1. **Using Sharp Tools:** When you're working with knives, scissors, or anything sharp, it's wise to have a parent supervise or assist you.

2. **Handling Hot Appliances:** If you're using the oven, stovetop, or microwave, it's a good idea to have an adult around, especially when you're first learning to use them.

3. **Dealing with Boiling Water:** When you're boiling water or making soups, parents can help you carry hot pots to the sink.

4. **Using Electrical Appliances:** Blenders, food processors, and mixers should be handled with care. Parents can show you how to use them safely.

5. **Managing Hot Oil:** Frying can be a bit tricky. Parents can help you with the hot oil and guide you on how to fry food safely.

Happy and safe cooking!

Remember young chefs, cooking is a wonderful skill that can be enjoyed for a lifetime. By following these safety tips and knowing when to ask for help, you'll always be a kitchen pro.

Food Allergies

Know Your Allergies: If you or someone you're cooking for has known food allergies, it's essential to be aware of them. Common allergies include nuts, dairy, eggs, wheat, soy, fish, and shellfish.

Ask for Guidance: When in doubt, ask a parent or guardian for help. They can guide you on ingredient substitutions and safe cooking practices to prevent allergic reactions.

Ingredient Check: Before you start cooking any recipe, take a good look at the ingredient list. If you spot an ingredient that you or someone you're cooking for is allergic to, it's time for a substitute.

Allergy-Friendly Substitutes: Many recipes can be adapted to accommodate allergies.

For example:
Dairy Allergy: Use dairy-free milk, cheese, or yogurt alternatives.

Egg Allergy: You can often replace eggs with applesauce, mashed bananas, or commercial egg replacers.

Nut Allergy: Skip the nuts or use seeds like sunflower or pumpkin seeds for a similar crunch.

Spice Sensitivity: Some spices can be potent, and people may have allergies or sensitivities to them.

Common allergenic spices include cinnamon, nutmeg, and paprika.

Always check with your parents or guardians about using these spices.

Label Reading: When buying packaged ingredients, read food labels carefully. Manufacturers are required to list common allergens in bold letters. This helps you spot potential allergens easily.

Food allergies are serious, but with a little caution and creativity, you can still enjoy cooking and sharing delicious meals with everyone. Cooking is about bringing people together, and being allergy-aware ensures that everyone can savor your culinary creations safely.

Happy and safe cooking!

Boiling the Macaroni

Let's kick things off with the main ingredient. The first step for each recipe is boiling macaroni. A great skill every chef should have in their apron pocket. So, grab your favorite pot, and let's get started!

Equipment:

- A large pot
- A stove or cooktop
- A wooden spoon or fork
- A colander (for draining)

Step 1: Prepare Your Pot

Grab a large pot, big enough to comfortably hold your macaroni with some extra space for the boiling bubbles.

Step 3: Add Water

Fill the pot with water. You'll need enough water to submerge the macaroni completely. Don't be shy; add a generous amount because pasta loves space to dance in.

Step 4: Season the Water (Pinch of Salt)

Here's a little secret to make your macaroni even tastier: add a pinch of salt to the water. It helps season the pasta from the inside out. But don't overdo it; a teaspoon or so should do the trick.

Step 5: Boil the Water

Place the pot on your stove or cooktop and turn the heat to high. We want that water to reach a rolling boil, where it's bubbling.

Step 6: Add the Macaroni

Once the water is boiling like a hot tub, carefully add your macaroni. Be gentle; you don't want any splashes!

Step 7: Stir Occasionally

Give your macaroni a gentle stir with a wooden spoon or fork. This helps prevent them from sticking together, ensuring you get perfectly cooked pasta.

Step 8: Cook to Al Dente

Check the cooking time on the macaroni package. Usually, it's around 7-8 minutes. Cook until your macaroni is "al dente," which means it's cooked but still slightly firm when you bite into it. Taste-testing is the best way to know when it's ready!

Step 9: Drain the Macaroni

Place a colander in your sink and carefully pour the macaroni into it to drain. Be cautious; that steam is hot!

To be safe ask your kitchen superhero (Mom, Dad or an Adult) to help you.

- Lift the pot with both hands and be sure to use oven mitts because the handles can be very hot.
- Pour away from yourself slowly to avoid any splashing.

Awesome Job Young Chefs!

Mac & Cheese Time!

Prep Work

Before you dive into the exciting recipes, let's explore a little bit on the fine art of prep work. This is where all the magic begins—the chopping, mincing, dicing, slicing, and cubing that transform ingredients into culinary wonders.

* And remember *"Safety First"* using Sharp Tools: When you're working with knives, scissors, or anything sharp, it's wise to have a parent supervise or assist you.

Chopping:

Chopping is all about cutting ingredients into irregular, bite-sized pieces. It's perfect for onions, bell peppers, or herbs.

Mincing:

Mincing is like the finer sibling of chopping. It creates tiny, uniform pieces of an ingredient, often used for garlic, ginger, or herbs.

Dicing:

Dicing is about creating uniform, small cubes. It's great for ingredients like tomatoes, onions, or carrots.

Slicing:

Slicing involves cutting ingredients into thin, flat pieces. Think cucumber rounds, zucchini slices.

Halving:

Halving is simple—cutting something in half to create two equal parts. It's often used for fruits like avocados or peaches or cherry tomatoes.

Cubing:

Cubing is all about creating, well, cubes! It's ideal for ingredients like cheese or cooked chicken.

Classic American Mac & Cheese

Ingredients

2 cups elbow macaroni

2 cups sharp cheddar cheese, shredded

1 ½ cups milk

¼ cup butter

¼ cup all-purpose flour

½ teaspoon salt

¼ teaspoon black pepper

¼ teaspoon paprika (optional, for a little kick)

✓ **Prepare Time**
10 Minutes

✓ **Cook Time**
20 Minutes

Hey there, little chefs! Welcome to our first stop on our Mac & Cheese World Adventure. We're starting with the all-time favorite: Classic American Mac & Cheese. It's creamy, cheesy, and oh-so-comforting.

Instructions

Step 1: Boil the Macaroni

Fill a large pot with water and add a pinch of salt. Bring the water to a boil over high heat.

Add the elbow macaroni and cook according to the package instructions (usually about 7-8 minutes). You want them to be "al dente," which means they're cooked but still a bit firm.

Drain the macaroni in a colander and set them aside.

Step 2: Make the Cheese Sauce

In the same pot you used for the macaroni, melt the butter over medium heat.

Once the butter is melted, add the flour and stir constantly for about 1-2 minutes. This will create a thick paste called a roux.

Gradually pour in the milk while whisking constantly to avoid lumps. Keep whisking until the mixture thickens, about 3-5 minutes. You should have a smooth sauce.

Add the shredded cheddar cheese, salt, black pepper, and paprika (if using). Stir until the cheese is completely melted and the sauce is smooth.

Step 3: Combine Macaroni and Cheese Sauce

Add the cooked macaroni to the cheese sauce. Stir well to coat the macaroni evenly with that creamy, cheesy goodness.

Cook for an additional 2-3 minutes, allowing the mac and cheese to meld together beautifully.

Serve and Enjoy

Your classic American Mac & Cheese is ready to be devoured! Scoop it into bowls, and if you'd like, sprinkle a little extra shredded cheese on top for an extra cheesy touch.

Gather your family or friends around the table, and dig in while it's still hot and gooey.

 Pro Tips:

- Want to make it even creamier? Use half-and-half or heavy cream instead of milk. Experiment with different cheeses like Monterey Jack, Gouda, or Swiss for unique flavor twists.
- Craving a crispy top? Pour your mac and cheese into a baking dish, sprinkle breadcrumbs mixed with melted butter on top, and bake it at 350°F (175°C) until golden brown.
- Don't forget to customize! Add diced ham, crispy bacon, or sautéed onions for an extra tasty twist.

There you go, lil chefs! You've just mastered the classic American Mac & Cheese. It's a dish that's loved all around the world for its creamy, cheesy goodness.

Enjoy your culinary creation and get ready for more mac and cheese adventures from different corners of the globe!

Italian Caprese Mac & Cheese

Ingredients

2 cups elbow macaroni

1 ½ cups fresh mozzarella cheese, diced

1 cup cherry tomatoes, halved

½ cup fresh basil leaves, torn

2 cloves garlic, minced

2 tablespoons extra- virgin olive oil

Salt and black pepper, to taste

Balsamic glaze (optional, for drizzling)

✓ **Prepare Time**
10 Minutes

✓ **Cook Time**
20 Minutes

Ciao, young chefs! Our Mac & Cheese World Adventure continues with a delightful Italian twist. Get ready to infuse the flavors of fresh tomatoes, mozzarella, and basil into your mac and cheese for a taste of Italy that'll make your taste buds sing!

Instructions

Step 1: Boil the Macaroni

Fill a large pot with water and add a pinch of salt. Bring the water to a boil over high heat.

Add the elbow macaroni and cook according to the package instructions until they are "al dente" (usually about 7-8 minutes).

Drain the macaroni in a colander and set them aside.

Step 2: Sauté the Garlic

In a large skillet, heat the olive oil over medium heat.

Add the minced garlic and sauté for about 30 seconds until it becomes fragrant, but be careful not to let it brown.

Step 3: Combine the Ingredients

Add the cooked macaroni to the skillet with the sautéed garlic.

Toss in the diced fresh mozzarella, cherry tomato halves, and torn basil leaves.

Season with a pinch of salt and a dash of black pepper.

Mix and Serve

Gently mix everything together in the skillet, allowing the mozzarella to melt slightly and create a creamy texture. Taste and adjust the seasoning if needed with more salt or pepper.

Garnish and Drizzle

Serve your Caprese Mac & Cheese in bowls.

For that extra Italian flair, drizzle a bit of balsamic glaze over the top before serving.

 Pro Tips:

- Fresh ingredients are key to this Italian-inspired dish, so try to use ripe, juicy tomatoes and fragrant basil for the best flavor.
- To make it even more indulgent, you can add a handful of grated Parmesan cheese or a dollop of ricotta cheese to the mix.
- Experiment with different pasta shapes – penne or rotini work great for holding all those delicious ingredients.

Buon appetito! You've just whipped up a taste of Italy with your Caprese Mac & Cheese. It's a harmony of flavors that will transport you straight to an Italian trattoria. Enjoy every bite, and get ready for more cheesy adventures from around the world!

Mexican Queso Fundido Mac & Cheese

Ingredients

2 cups elbow macaroni

1 cup Mexican chorizo, casing removed and crumbled

2 cups shredded Monterey Jack cheese

1 cup shredded cheddar cheese

1 cup diced tomatoes 1/2 cup diced red onion

1/4 cup chopped fresh cilantro

1/4 cup pickled jalapeño slices (adjust to your spice preference)

2 cloves garlic, minced 1 tablespoon vegetable oil

Salt and black pepper, to taste

Lime wedges for garnish (optional)

✓ **Prepare Time**
   10 Minutes

✓ **Cook Time**
   20 Minutes

Hola, little chefs! We're spicing things up on our Mac & Cheese World Adventure with a Mexican twist - Queso Fundido Mac & Cheese. Get ready for a cheesy, gooey, and slightly spicy delight that'll have you saying "Olé!" Let's dive in.

Instructions

Step 1: Boil the Macaroni

Start by boiling a large pot of water and adding a pinch of salt.

Once the water is boiling, add the elbow macaroni and cook according to the package instructions until they're "al dente" (usually about 7-8 minutes).

Drain the macaroni in a colander and set them aside.

Step 2: Cook the Chorizo

In a large skillet over medium-high heat, add the vegetable oil.

Crumble the Mexican chorizo into the skillet and cook it, breaking it apart with a spatula as it cooks, until it's browned and cooked through, about 5-7 minutes.

Step 3: Combine the Ingredients

In a large mixing bowl, combine the cooked macaroni, cooked chorizo, diced tomatoes, diced red onion, minced garlic, and pickled jalapeño slices.

Toss everything together until they're evenly distributed.

Step 4: Add the Cheeses

Sprinkle the shredded Monterey Jack cheese and shredded cheddar cheese over the macaroni mixture.

Stir well to combine, allowing the cheeses to melt and create a gooey, creamy sauce.

Garnish and Serve

Once the cheese is fully melted and everything is well mixed, sprinkle fresh cilantro over the top.

Taste and adjust the seasoning with salt and black pepper as needed.

If you like it extra zesty, squeeze a lime wedge over your Queso Fundido Mac & Cheese before digging in.

Pro Tips:

- If you can't find Mexican chorizo, you can substitute it with ground beef or pork seasoned with taco seasoning.
- Customize the spiciness by adding more or fewer jalapeño slices.
- For a smoky twist, conzzzsider adding a pinch of smoked paprika or chipotle powder.

¡Buen provecho! You've just created a fiesta of flavors with your Queso Fundido Mac & Cheese. The cheesy, spicy goodness is like a celebration on your taste buds. Enjoy every bite, and get ready for more global mac and cheese adventures!

Japanese Miso Mac & Cheese

Ingredients

2 cups elbow macaroni

2 cups shredded Japanese or regular cheddar cheese

1/4 cup unsalted butter

1/4 cup all-purpose flour

2 cups whole milk

2 tablespoons white miso paste

1/4 cup sliced green onions (for garnish)

1 sheet of nori seaweed, crumbled (optional, for garnish)

Salt and black pepper, to taste

A pinch of sesame seeds (optional, for garnish)

✔ **Prepare Time**
20 Minutes

✔ **Prepare Time**
30 Minutes

Konnichiwa, young chefs! We're on a flavorful journey through Japan with our Miso Mac & Cheese. This dish brings together the umami richness of miso paste and the comfort of mac and cheese. Get your taste buds ready for a delicious adventure!

Instructions

Step 1: Boil the Macaroni

Start by boiling a large pot of water and adding a pinch of salt.

Once the water is boiling, add the elbow macaroni and cook according to the package instructions until they're "al dente" (usually about 7-8 minutes).

Drain the macaroni in a colander and set them aside.

Step 2: Make the Miso Cheese Sauce

In a separate saucepan over medium heat, melt the butter.

Once melted, add the flour and whisk constantly for about 1-2 minutes to create a roux (a thick paste).

Gradually pour in the whole milk while whisking continuously until the mixture thickens, usually about 3-5 minutes.

Reduce the heat to low and add the shredded cheese, one handful at a time, stirring until it's fully melted and the sauce is smooth.

Stir in the white miso paste until it's well combined and the sauce has a beautiful miso flavor.

Step 3: Combine Macaroni and Miso Cheese Sauce

Add the cooked macaroni to the miso cheese sauce and stir until the macaroni is evenly coated in the creamy, cheesy miso goodness.

Season with salt and black pepper to taste.

Garnish and Serve

Spoon your Miso Mac & Cheese into bowls, and garnish with sliced green onions, crumbled nori seaweed, and a pinch of sesame seeds if you'd like.

Dive into your bowl of Japanese comfort food!

 **Pro Tips:**

- White miso paste is milder than red miso, so it works best for this dish. You can find it in the Asian section of most grocery stores.
- To add a protein punch, consider topping your Miso Mac & Cheese with grilled chicken or sautéed tofu.
- Want a little extra kick? Sprinkle on some shichimi togarashi (Japanese seven spice) for some heat.

Oishii (delicious)! Your Miso Mac & Cheese is a delightful fusion of Japanese and American comfort foods. The umami from the miso paste adds a unique depth of flavor. Enjoy every bite, and get ready for more exciting mac and cheese adventures from around the world!

French Ratatouille Mac & Cheese

Ingredients

For the Mac & Cheese:

2 cups elbow macaroni

2 cups grated Gruyère cheese

1 cup grated Parmesan cheese

1 ½ cups whole milk

1/4 cup unsalted butter

1/4 cup all-purpose flour

Salt and black pepper to taste

For the Ratatouille:

1 medium eggplant, diced into small cubes

1 zucchini, diced

1/4 onion, finely chopped

2 cloves garlic, minced

2 tablespoons olive oil

1 can (14 oz) crushed tomatoes

1 teaspoon dried thyme

1 teaspoon dried basil

Salt and black pepper to taste

Fresh basil leaves, for garnish

Prepare Time
30 Minutes

Cook Time
60 Minutes

Bonjour, les petite chefs! We're about to embark on a culinary journey to France with our Ratatouille Mac & Cheese. This delightful dish combines the rustic charm of French cuisine with the creamy comfort of mac and cheese. Let's dive in and create something magnifique!

Instructions

Step 1: Roast the Vegetables

Preheat your oven to 400°F (200°C).

Spread the diced eggplant and zucchini on a baking sheet.

Drizzle olive oil over the vegetables and season with salt and black pepper.

Roast them in the preheated oven for about 20-25 minutes or until they become tender and slightly caramelized.

Step 2: Boil the Macaroni

While the vegetables are roasting, fill a large pot with water and add a pinch of salt.

Bring the water to a boil over high heat.

Add the elbow macaroni and cook according to the package instructions until they're "al dente" (usually about 7-8 minutes).

Drain the macaroni in a colander and set them aside.

Step 3: Make the Ratatouille

In a large skillet, heat some olive oil over medium heat.

Add the finely chopped onion and sauté for about 3-4 minutes until it becomes translucent.

Step 3: Make the Ratatouille (Continued)

Stir in the minced garlic and cook for an additional minute until fragrant.

Add the roasted vegetables, crushed tomatoes, dried thyme, and dried basil to the skillet.

Season with salt and black pepper to taste.

Simmer the ratatouille mixture for about 10-15 minutes to allow the flavors to meld together.

Step 4: Make the Cheese Sauce

In a separate saucepan over medium heat, melt the butter.

Once melted, add the flour and whisk continuously for about 1-2 minutes to create a roux (thick paste).

Gradually pour in the whole milk while whisking continuously until the mixture thickens, usually about 3-5 minutes.

Reduce the heat to low and add the grated Gruyère cheese and grated Parmesan cheese, stirring until the cheese is fully melted and the sauce is smooth.

Step 5: Combine Macaroni, Ratatouille, and Cheese Sauce

Add the cooked macaroni to the cheese sauce and stir until the macaroni is evenly coated.

Then, gently fold in the ratatouille mixture, making sure to distribute the roasted vegetables throughout the mac and cheese.

Garnish and Serve

Spoon your Ratatouille Mac & Cheese into bowls, and garnish with fresh basil leaves.

Serve hot and savor the marriage of French rustic flavors and creamy mac and cheese.

 Pro Tips:

- Ratatouille is a versatile dish, so feel free to add or substitute vegetables like mushrooms, yellow squash, or cherry tomatoes to your liking.
- For more garlic flavor, roast the garlic halves with the other vegetables.
- If you want a hint of spice, add a pinch of red pepper flakes to the ratatouille.
- Craving an extra crispy top? Sprinkle breadcrumbs mixed with melted butter over your Ratatouille Mac & Cheese and bake it at 350°F (175°C) until golden brown.

Voilà! Your Ratatouille Mac & Cheese is a culinary masterpiece that captures the essence of French cuisine. The roasted veggies and creamy cheese sauce make it a delight for the senses. Enjoy every bite, and get ready for more mac and cheese adventures from around the world!

Indian Tikka Masala Mac & Cheese

Ingredients

For the Mac & Cheese:

2 cups elbow macaroni

2 cups shredded sharp cheddar cheese

1 cup heavy cream

1/4 cup unsalted butter

Salt and black pepper to taste

For the Tikka Masala Sauce:

1 cup tomato puree

1/2 cup heavy cream

2 tablespoons vegetable oil

1 small onion, finely chopped

2 cloves garlic, minced

1 tablespoon ginger paste

2 tablespoons Tikka Masala spice blend

1 teaspoon paprika (for color and a mild kick)

Salt and black pepper to taste

Fresh cilantro leaves, for garnish

 **Prepare Time**
20 Minutes

 **Cook Time**
30 Minutes

Namaste, young chefs! Today, we're blending the rich and spicy flavors of India with the comforting goodness of mac and cheese to create Tikka Masala Mac & Cheese. Get ready to embark on a mouthwatering journey through the vibrant spices of Indian cuisine.

Instructions

Step 1: Boil the Macaroni

Fill a large pot with water and add a pinch of salt.

Bring the water to a boil over high heat.

Add the elbow macaroni and cook according to the package instructions until they're "al dente" (usually about 7-8 minutes).

Drain the macaroni in a colander and set them aside.

Step 2: Make the Tikka Masala Sauce

In a separate skillet or saucepan, heat the vegetable oil over medium heat.

Add the finely chopped onion and sauté until it becomes translucent, about 3-4 minutes.

Stir in the minced garlic and ginger paste, and cook for an additional 1-2 minutes until fragrant.

Add the Tikka Masala spice blend and paprika. Stir well to combine.

Pour in the tomato puree and heavy cream, stirring continuously.

Season the sauce with salt and black pepper to taste.

Simmer the sauce for about 5-7 minutes until it thickens and the flavors meld together.

Step 3: Combine Macaroni and Tikka Masala Sauce

Add the cooked macaroni to the Tikka Masala sauce, and gently toss them together until the macaroni is coated with the spicy, creamy goodness.

Step 4: Add Cheese and Cream

Sprinkle the shredded sharp cheddar cheese over the macaroni.

Pour in the heavy cream.

Stir everything well until the cheese melts and the sauce becomes wonderfully creamy.

Garnish and Serve

Spoon your Tikka Masala Mac & Cheese into bowls.

Garnish with fresh cilantro leaves for a burst of color and flavor.

Serve hot and savor the exotic blend of Indian spices with the comfort of mac and cheese.

 Pro Tips:

- Tikka Masala spice blends are available in most grocery stores, or you can make your own by combining spices like coriander, cumin, paprika, and garam masala.
- If you like it spicier, add a pinch of cayenne pepper or some chopped green chilies to the sauce.
- For a protein boost, you can add cooked chicken or paneer cubes to make it a complete meal.

Delicious! Your Tikka Masala Mac & Cheese is a mouthwatering fusion of two culinary worlds. The spicy, creamy sauce takes mac and cheese to a whole new level. Enjoy every bite, and get ready for more exciting mac and cheese adventures from around the world!

Greek Mediterranean Mac & Cheese

Ingredients

For the Mac & Cheese:

2 cups elbow macaroni

2 cups crumbled feta cheese

1 ½ cups whole milk

1/4 cup unsalted butter

1/4 cup all-purpose flour

Salt and black pepper to taste

For the Mediterranean Topping:

1 cup diced tomatoes

1/2 cup diced cucumber

1/2 cup pitted Kalamata olives, chopped

1/4 cup finely chopped red onion

1/4 cup chopped fresh parsley

2 tablespoons extra- virgin olive oil

1 tablespoon red wine vinegar

Salt and black pepper to taste

 **Prepare Time**
20 Minutes

 **Cook Time**
30 Minutes

Yasou, young chefs! We're setting sail for Greece on our Mac & Cheese World Adventure with a Mediterranean twist - Greek Mediterranean Mac & Cheese. This dish combines the flavors of Greece with the creamy comfort of mac and cheese. Opa! Let's dive into this delicious journey.

Instructions

Step 1: Boil the Macaroni

Start by boiling a large pot of water and adding a pinch of salt.

Add the elbow macaroni and cook according to the package instructions until they're "al dente" (usually about 7-8 minutes).

Drain the macaroni in a colander and set them aside.

Step 2: Make the Mediterranean Topping

In a mixing bowl, combine the diced tomatoes, diced cucumber, chopped Kalamata olives, finely chopped red onion, and chopped fresh parsley.

Drizzle extra-virgin olive oil and red wine vinegar over the mixture.

Season with salt and black pepper to taste.

Toss everything together to create a refreshing Mediterranean topping. Set it aside.

Step 3: Make the Cheese Sauce

In a saucepan over medium heat, melt the butter.

Once melted, add the flour and whisk continuously for about 1-2 minutes to create a roux (a thick paste).

Gradually pour in the whole milk while whisking continuously until the mixture thickens, usually about 3-5 minutes.

Step 3: Make the Cheese Sauce (Continued)

Season with salt and black pepper to taste.

Reduce the heat to low and add the crumbled feta cheese, stirring until the cheese is fully melted and the sauce is smooth.

Step 4: Combine Macaroni and Cheese Sauce

Add the cooked macaroni to the feta cheese sauce and stir until the macaroni is evenly coated with the creamy, tangy goodness.

Serve and Top with Mediterranean Topping

Spoon your Greek Mediterranean Mac & Cheese into bowls.

Top each serving generously with the refreshing Mediterranean topping you prepared earlier.

Get ready for a taste of Greece!

 Pro Tips:

- For a touch of heat, sprinkle some red pepper flakes over your mac and cheese

- Want to add some protein? Grilled chicken or shrimp pairs wonderfully with this dish.
- For an extra Mediterranean twist, you can add a pinch of dried oregano or some crumbled Greek feta cheese on top.

Kali orexi (good appetite)! Your Greek Mediterranean Mac & Cheese is a delightful fusion of Greek flavors and creamy mac and cheese. The tangy feta cheese and fresh Mediterranean topping make it a taste of the Aegean.

Australian Vegemite Mac & Cheese

G'day, young chefs! Our Mac & Cheese World Adventure takes us down under to Australia with a uniquely Aussie twist - Vegemite Mac & Cheese. Get ready for a savory, salty, and oh-so-Aussie mac and cheese that's sure to be a hit. Let's give it a burl!

Ingredients

For the Mac & Cheese:

2 cups elbow macaroni

2 cups shredded sharp chedder cheese

1 cup whole milk

1/4 cup unsalted butter

Salt and black pepper to taste

For the Vegemite Sauce:

2 tablespoons Vegemite

1/4 cup hot water

2 tablespoons unsalted butter

2 tablespoons all- purpose flour

1/4 cup grated Parmesan cheese

1/4 cup sour cream

Salt and black pepper, to taste.

For the Garnish:

Diced Avacado DicedTomato

Chopped Chives

Prepare Time
20 Minutes

Cook Time
30 Minutes

Instructions

Step 1: Boil the Macaroni

Fill a large pot with water and add a pinch of salt. Bring the water to a boil over high heat.

Add the elbow macaroni and cook according to the package instructions until they're "al dente" (usually about 7-8 minutes).

Drain the macaroni in a colander and set them aside.

Step 2: Make the Vegemite Sauce

In a small bowl, mix the Vegemite and hot water together until the Vegemite is dissolved. Set it aside.

In a saucepan over medium heat, melt the butter.

Once melted, add the flour and whisk continuously for about 1-2 minutes to create a roux (a thick paste).

Gradually pour in the whole milk while whisking continuously until the mixture thickens, usually about 3-5 minutes.

Season with salt and black pepper to taste.

Reduce the heat to low and add the grated Parmesan cheese, stirring until the cheese is fully melted and the sauce is smooth.

Stir in the Vegemite mixture until it's well combined with the cheese sauce.

Finally, add the sour cream and continue stirring until the sauce is creamy and well mixed.

Step 3: Combine Macaroni and Vegemite Sauce

Add the cooked macaroni to the Vegemite cheese sauce and stir until the macaroni is evenly coated with the unique Vegemite flavor.

Garnish and Serve

Spoon your Vegemite Mac & Cheese into bowls.

Add diced tomatos and avacado and sprinkle chopped chives.

Get ready to savor the bold and distinctive taste of Australia with every bite!

 Pro Tips:

- Vegemite is quite salty, so go easy on the salt when seasoning your mac and cheese.
- Serve your Vegemite Mac & Cheese with a sprinkle of crispy bacon bits for an extra Aussie touch.
- For some added texture and flavor, try mixing in some sautéed onions or diced mushrooms.

Too easy! Your Vegemite Mac & Cheese is a true-blue Aussie delight. The rich, savory Vegemite sauce adds a unique twist to the classic mac and cheese. Enjoy every bite, and get ready for more mac and cheese adventures from around the world! Cheers!

Thai Green Curry
Mac & Cheese

Ingredients

For the Mac & Cheese:

2 cups elbow macaroni

2 cups shredded mozzarella cheese

1 cup coconut milk

1/4 cup unsalted butter

Salt and black pepper to taste

For the Thai Green Curry Sauce:

2 tablespoons Thai green curry paste

1 can (13.5 oz) coconut milk

1 tablespoon vegetable oil

1 red bell pepper, thinly sliced

1 zucchini, thinly sliced

1 cup sliced mushrooms

1 tablespoon fish sauce (or soy sauce for a vegetarian option)

1 teaspoon brown sugar

Juice of 1 lime

Fresh cilantro leaves, for garnish

Lime wedges, for serving

 Prepare Time
20 Minutes

 Cook Time
30 Minutes

Sawasdee, young chefs! We're taking a flavorful trip to Thailand on our Mac & Cheese World Adventure with a tantalizing twist - Thai Green Curry Mac & Cheese. This fusion of creamy comfort and exotic Thai flavors will transport your taste buds to the streets of Bangkok. Let's dive in and create a culinary masterpiece!

Instructions

Step 1: Boil the Macaroni

Start by boiling a large pot of water and adding a pinch of salt.

Once the water is boiling, add the elbow macaroni and cook according to the package instructions until they're "al dente" (usually about 7-8 minutes).

Drain the macaroni in a colander and set them aside.

Step 2: Make the Thai Green Curry Sauce

In a large skillet or wok, heat the vegetable oil over medium heat.

Add the Thai green curry paste and cook for about 1-2 minutes until it becomes fragrant.

Pour in the coconut milk and stir well to combine with the curry paste.

Add the thinly sliced red bell pepper, zucchini, and sliced mushrooms to the skillet.

Stir-fry the vegetables for about 5-7 minutes until they're tender but still crisp.

Season with fish sauce (or soy sauce for a vegetarian option) and brown sugar.

Step 2: (Continued)

Squeeze in the juice of one lime and mix everything together.

Remove the skillet from heat.

Step 3: Make the Cheese Sauce

In a separate saucepan over medium heat, melt the butter.

Once melted, add a pinch of salt and black pepper.

Pour in the coconut milk and stir until it's heated through.

Reduce the heat to low and add the shredded mozzarella cheese, stirring until the cheese is fully melted and the sauce is smooth.

Step 4: Combine Macaroni and Cheese Sauce

Add the cooked macaroni to the cheese sauce and stir until the macaroni is evenly coated with the creamy coconut goodness.

Then, gently fold in the Thai green curry sauce, making sure to distribute the Thai vegetables throughout the mac and cheese.

Garnish and Serve

Spoon your Thai Green Curry Mac & Cheese into bowls.

Garnish with fresh cilantro leaves and serve with lime wedges on the side for an extra zesty kick.

 Pro Tips:

- Thai green curry paste can vary in spiciness, so adjust the amount to your heat preference.
- To make it heartier, consider adding cooked chicken or tofu to your Thai Green Curry Mac & Cheese.
- For some extra crunch, sprinkle crushed peanuts on top before serving.

Aroy mak mak (very delicious)! Your Thai Green Curry Mac & Cheese is a mouthwatering blend of creamy comfort and Thai spice. The fragrant curry sauce and zesty lime take this dish to a whole new level. Enjoy every bite, and get ready for more mac and cheese adventures from around the world!

Brazilian Feijoada Mac & Cheese

Ingredients

For the Mac & Cheese:

2 cups elbow macaroni

2 cups shredded mozzarella cheese

1 cup whole milk

1/4 cup unsalted butter

Salt and black pepper to taste

For the Feijoada Topping:

1 can (15 oz) black beans, drained and rinsed

1/2 lb smoked sausage (linguiça), sliced into rounds

1/2 lb smoked pork shoulder (paio or smoked ham), cubed

1/2 cup diced onion

2 cloves garlic, minced

2 bay leaves

1 tablespoon vegetable oil

Salt and black pepper, to taste

Chopped fresh Cilantro, for garnish

Orange wedges, for serving (traditional accompaniment)

Prepare Time
20 Minutes

Cook Time
30 Minutes

Olá, young chefs! We're embarking on a culinary journey to Brazil with a fusion that combines the rich, hearty flavors of Brazilian Feijoada with the creamy comfort of mac and cheese. Get ready to savor the soulful delights of Brazilian cuisine!

Instructions

Step 1: Boil the Macaroni

Fill a large pot with water and add a pinch of salt. Bring the water to a boil over high heat.

Add the elbow macaroni and cook according to the package instructions until they're "al dente" (usually about 7-8 minutes).

Drain the macaroni in a colander and set them aside.

Step 2: Prepare the Feijoada Topping

In a large skillet, heat the vegetable oil over medium heat.

Add the diced onion and sauté for about 3-4 minutes until it becomes translucent.

Stir in the minced garlic and cook for an additional 1-2 minutes until fragrant.

Add the sliced smoked sausage and cubed smoked pork shoulder to the skillet.

Sauté for about 5-7 minutes until they're slightly browned. Pour in the black beans and add the bay leaves.

Season with salt and black pepper to taste.

Let the Feijoada mixture simmer for about 10-15 minutes to allow the flavors to meld together. Remove the bay leaves.

Step 3: Make the Cheese Sauce

In a separate saucepan over medium heat, melt the butter. Once melted, add a pinch of salt and black pepper.

Pour in the whole milk and stir until it's heated through.

Reduce the heat to low and add the shredded mozzarella cheese, stirring until the cheese is fully melted and the sauce is smooth.

Step 4: Combine Macaroni and Feijoada

Add the cooked macaroni to the cheese sauce and stir until the macaroni is evenly coated with the creamy goodness.

Then, gently fold in the Feijoada mixture, making sure to distribute the black beans and smoked meats throughout the mac and cheese.

Garnish and Serve

Spoon your Feijoada Mac & Cheese into bowls. Garnish with chopped fresh cilantro.

Serve hot with orange wedges on the side, as is tradition in Brazil.

 Pro Tips:

- For extra authenticity, serve your Feijoada Mac & Cheese with a side of farofa (toasted cassava flour) and collard greens.
- Feijoada is traditionally made with pork, but you can make it vegetarian by omitting the meats and using vegetable stock instead.
- If you can't find Brazilian sausages, you can use smoked sausage or chorizo as a substitute.

Bom apetite (enjoy your meal)! Your Feijoada Mac & Cheese is a delightful blend of creamy comfort and the rich, savory flavors of Brazil. The feijoada topping adds depth and heartiness to this dish. Enjoy every bite, and get ready for more mac and cheese adventures from around the world!

Russian Borscht Mac & Cheese

Ingredients

For the Mac & Cheese:

2 cups elbow macaroni

2 cups shredded sharp cheddar cheese

1 cup whole milk

1/4 cup unsalted butter

Salt and black pepper to taste

For the Borscht Topping:

1 large beet, peeled and diced

1 cup shredded cabbage

1 cup diced potatoes

1/2 cup diced carrots

1/2 cup diced onion

2 cloves garlic, minced

2 tablespoons vegetable oil

4 cups vegetable or beef broth

2 tablespoons tomato paste

1 bay leaf

1 teaspoon dried dill

Salt and black pepper to taste

Sour cream, for garnish (optional)

Prepare Time
20 Minutes

Cook Time
30 Minutes

Здравствуйте, young chefs! Our Mac & Cheese World Adventure continues in Russia with a comforting fusion dish - Russian Borscht Mac & Cheese. We're blending the heartwarming flavors of borscht, a beloved Russian soup, with the creamy goodness of mac and cheese. Let's dive into this delightful culinary journey!

Instructions

Step 1: Boil the Macaroni

Start by boiling a large pot of water and adding a pinch of salt.

Once the water is boiling, add the elbow macaroni and cook according to the package instructions until they're "al dente" (usually about 7-8 minutes).

Drain the macaroni in a colander and set them aside.

Step 2: Prepare the Borscht Topping

In a large soup pot, heat the vegetable oil over medium heat.

Add the diced onion and sauté for about 3-4 minutes until it becomes translucent.

Stir in the minced garlic and cook for an additional 1-2 minutes until fragrant.

Add the diced potatoes, diced carrots, and diced beet to the pot.

Sauté for about 5-7 minutes until the vegetables begin to soften.

Pour in the vegetable or beef broth and add the shredded cabbage, bay leaf, dried dill, and tomato paste.

Step 2: Prepare the Borscht Topping (Continued)

Season with salt and black pepper to taste.

Let the borscht simmer for about 20-25 minutes until all the vegetables are tender and the flavors meld together. Remove the bay leaf.

Step 3: Make the Cheese Sauce

In a separate saucepan over medium heat, melt the butter. Once melted, add a pinch of salt and black pepper.

Pour in the whole milk and stir until it's heated through.

Reduce the heat to low and add the shredded sharp cheddar cheese, stirring until the cheese is fully melted and the sauce is smooth.

Step 4: Combine Macaroni and Borscht

Add the cooked macaroni to the cheese sauce and stir until the macaroni is evenly coated with the creamy goodness.

Then, gently fold in the borscht mixture, making sure to distribute the colorful vegetables throughout the mac and cheese.

Garnish and Serve

Spoon your Borscht Mac & Cheese into bowls.

If you like, garnish with a dollop of sour cream for that traditional Russian touch. Get ready to enjoy the comforting flavors of Russia in every bite!

 **Pro Tips:**

- Add cooked beef, chicken, or even beans to your Borscht Mac & Cheese for extra protein.
- Borscht traditionally has a touch of vinegar for tanginess.
- For an extra Russian touch, serve with a slice of dark rye bread.

Приятного аппетита (enjoy your meal), young chefs! Your Borscht Mac & Cheese is a wonderful fusion of creamy comfort and the hearty flavors of Russian borscht. The colorful vegetables and cheesy goodness make this dish truly special. Enjoy !

Jamaican Jerk Mac & Cheese

Ingredients

For the Mac & Cheese:

2 cups elbow macaroni

2 cups shredded pepper jack cheese

1 cup whole milk

1/4 cup unsalted butter

Salt and black pepper, to taste

For the Jamaican Jerk Topping:

1 lb boneless chicken thighs, cut into bite- sized pieces

2 tablespoons Jamaican jerk seasoning

2 tablespoons vegetable oil

1 red bell pepper, diced

1 green bell pepper, diced

1 onion, diced

2 cloves garlic, minced

1 can (14 oz) diced tomatoes

1 tablespoon brown sugar

Salt and black pepper to taste

Fresh cilantro leaves, for garnish

Prepare Time
20 Minutes

Cook Time
30 Minutes

Young chefs! We're taking a flavorful journey to the Caribbean with a spicy twist - Jamaican Jerk Mac & Cheese. Get ready for a fusion of creamy comfort and the bold, fiery flavors of Jamaican jerk seasoning. Let's dive into this island-inspired culinary creation!

Instructions

Step 1: Boil the Macaroni

Fill a large pot with water and add a pinch of salt. Bring the water to a boil over high heat.

Add the elbow macaroni and cook according to the package instructions until they're "al dente" (usually about 7-8 minutes).

Drain the macaroni in a colander and set them aside.

Step 2: Prepare the Jamaican Jerk Topping

In a mixing bowl, combine the Jamaican jerk seasoning with the vegetable oil to create a marinade.

Toss the bite-sized chicken pieces in the jerk marinade, ensuring they're well coated.

In a large skillet or pan, heat some oil over medium-high heat.

Add the marinated chicken and sauté until it's browned and cooked through, usually about 5-7 minutes.

Remove the cooked chicken from the skillet and set it aside.

Then, gently fold in the Jamaican jerk topping, making sure to distribute the flavorful chicken and vegetables throughout the mac and cheese.

Step 2: (Continued)

In the same skillet, add diced red and green bell peppers, diced onion, and minced garlic.

Sauté for about 3-4 minutes until the vegetables are tender. Stir in the diced tomatoes, brown sugar, and cooked chicken. Season with salt and black pepper to taste.

Let the Jamaican jerk topping simmer for about 5-7 minutes to meld the flavors together.

Step 3: Make the Cheese Sauce

In a separate saucepan over medium heat, melt the butter. Once melted, add a pinch of salt and black pepper.

Pour in the whole milk and stir until it's heated through.

Reduce the heat to low and add the shredded pepper jack cheese, stirring until the cheese is fully melted and the sauce is smooth.

Step 4: Combine Macaroni and Jamaican Jerk Topping

Add the cooked macaroni to the cheese sauce and stir until the macaroni is evenly coated with the creamy pepper jack goodness.

Garnish and Serve

Spoon your Jamaican Jerk Mac & Cheese into bowls.

Garnish with fresh cilantro leaves for a burst of color and flavor.

Pro Tips:

- Adjust the level of heat by adding more or less Jamaican jerk seasoning to suit your taste.
- You can use shrimp or tofu instead of chicken for a delicious twist.
- Serve with a wedge of lime for an extra zesty kick.

Your Jamaican Jerk Mac & Cheese is a harmonious blend of creamy comfort and the fiery flavors of the Caribbean. The spicy chicken and pepper jack cheese make it a true island delight.

Get ready to experience the vibrant taste of Jamaica with every spicy bite!

Egyptian Koshari Mac & Cheese

Ingredients

For the Mac & Cheese:

2 cups elbow macaroni

2 cups shredded mozzarella cheese

1 cup whole milk

1/4 cup unsalted butter

Salt and black pepper to taste

For the Koshari Topping:

1 cup dried brown lentils

1 cup long-grain white rice

2 cups water

2 tablespoons vegetable oil

1 onion, thinly sliced

2 cloves garlic, minced

1 can (14 oz) diced tomatoes

1 tablespoon ground cumin

1 tablespoon ground coriander

Salt and black pepper to taste

Red pepper flakes, for a spicy kick (optional)

Crispy fried onions, for garnish (optional)

Fresh cilantro leaves, for garnish

 **Prepare Time**
30 Minutes

 **Cook Time**
60 Minutes

Marhaba, young chefs! We're on an exotic adventure to Egypt with a fusion that combines the heartiness of Koshari, a beloved Egyptian street food, with the creamy comfort of mac and cheese. Get ready to enjoy the flavors of the Nile in our Koshari Mac & Cheese!

Instructions

Step 1: Boil the Macaroni

Start by boiling a large pot of water and adding a pinch of salt.

Once the water is boiling, add the elbow macaroni and cook according to the package instructions until they're "al dente" (usually about 7-8 minutes).

Drain the macaroni in a colander and set them aside.

Step 2: Prepare the Koshari Topping

1. Rinse the brown lentils under cold water and drain them.

2. In a saucepan, combine the lentils and 2 cups of water. Bring to a boil, then reduce the heat to low, cover, and simmer for about 20-25 minutes until the lentils are tender but not mushy. Drain any excess water.

3. In a separate pot, cook the white rice according to package instructions until it's fluffy and cooked through.

4. In a large skillet, heat the vegetable oil over medium heat.

5. Add the thinly sliced onion and sauté for about 5-7 minutes until they turn golden brown and crispy. Remove half of the crispy onions and set them aside for garnish.

6. Stir in the minced garlic and cook for an additional 1-2 minutes until fragrant.

Step 2: Prepare the Koshari Topping (Continued)

7. Add the diced tomatoes (with their juice) to the skillet.

8. Season with ground cumin, ground coriander, salt, black pepper, and red pepper flakes (if you like it spicy).

9. Let the tomato mixture simmer for about 5-7 minutes until it thickens and the flavors meld together.

Step 3: Make the Cheese Sauce

In a separate saucepan over medium heat, melt the butter. Once melted, add a pinch of salt and black pepper.

Pour in the whole milk and stir until it's heated through.

Reduce the heat to low and add the shredded mozzarella cheese, stirring until the cheese is fully melted and the sauce is smooth.

Step 4: Combine Macaroni and Koshari Topping

Add the cooked macaroni to the cheese sauce and stir until the macaroni is evenly coated with the creamy goodness.

Then, gently fold in the Koshari mixture, combining the flavorful lentils, rice, and tomato sauce throughout the mac and cheese.

Garnish and Serve

Spoon your Koshari Mac & Cheese into bowls.

Garnish with the reserved crispy fried onions and fresh cilantro leaves for a burst of flavor and texture.

 **Pro Tips:**

- You can add some cooked chickpeas or top your Koshari Mac & Cheese with crispy falafel for a delightful twist.
- For an authentic touch, serve with a side of Egyptian garlic tomato sauce or hot sauce.
- Koshari is traditionally served with a splash of vinegar; you can try this on your Mac & Cheese if you like a tangy kick.

Sahteen (enjoy your meal), young chefs! Your Koshari Mac & Cheese is a fusion of creamy comfort and the flavors of Egyptian street food. The lentils, rice, and crispy onions add a unique texture and depth of flavor to this dish. Enjoy!

Korean Kimchi Mac & Cheese

Ingredients

For the Mac & Cheese:

2 cups elbow macaroni

2 cups shredded sharp cheddar cheese

1 cup whole milk

1/4 cup unsalted butter

Salt and black pepper to taste

For the Kimchi Topping:

1 cup kimchi chopped (you can find it in most grocery stores or make your own)

2 tablespoons sesame oil

1 tablespoon gochugaru (Korean red pepper flakes, adjust to taste)

2 cloves garlic, minced

1 tablespoon soy sauce

1 tablespoon brown sugar

1/2 cup thinly sliced scallions (green parts)

Sesame seeds, for garnish

Nori (seaweed) strips, for garnish

 **Prepare Time**
10 Minutes

 **Cook Time**
20 Minutes

Annyeong, young chefs! We're heading to South Korea on our Mac & Cheese World Adventure with a twist that combines the tangy and spicy flavors of kimchi with the creamy comfort of mac and cheese. Get ready for a flavor explosion in our Korean Kimchi Mac & Cheese!

Instructions

Step 1: Boil the Macaroni

Fill a large pot with water and add a pinch of salt.

Bring the water to a boil over high heat.

Add the elbow macaroni and cook according to the package instructions until they're "al dente" (usually about 7-8 minutes).

Drain the macaroni in a colander and set them aside.

Step 2: Prepare the Kimchi Topping

In a skillet or pan, heat the sesame oil over medium heat.

Add the minced garlic and sauté for about 1-2 minutes until fragrant.

Stir in the chopped kimchi and gochugaru (Korean red pepper flakes). Cook for another 3-4 minutes until the kimchi is heated through and slightly caramelized.

Add the soy sauce and brown sugar, stirring to combine.

Toss in the thinly sliced scallions (green parts) and cook for an additional 2 minutes until they're wilted and fragrant.

Step 3: Make the Cheese Sauce

In a separate saucepan over medium heat, melt the butter.

Once melted, add a pinch of salt and black pepper.

Pour in the whole milk and stir until it's heated through.

Reduce the heat to low and add the shredded sharp cheddar cheese, stirring until the cheese is fully melted and the sauce is smooth.

Step 4: Combine Macaroni and Kimchi Topping

Add the cooked macaroni to the cheese sauce and stir until the macaroni is evenly coated with the creamy goodness.

Then, gently fold in the kimchi mixture, ensuring that the spicy and tangy flavors are distributed throughout the mac and cheese.

Garnish and Serve

Spoon your Korean Kimchi Mac & Cheese into bowls.

Garnish with sesame seeds and nori (seaweed) strips for added Korean flair.

 **Pro Tips:**

- Top your Korean Kimchi Mac & Cheese with a fried egg for an extra burst of flavor and texture.
- Adjust the level of spice to your liking by adding more or less gochugaru.
- If you enjoy a richer flavor, try using aged kimchi.

맛있게 드세요 (enjoy your meal)! Your Korean Kimchi Mac & Cheese is a delightful blend of creamy comfort and the bold, spicy flavors of Korea. The kimchi adds a tangy kick that pairs perfectly with the cheesy goodness.

Moroccan Tagine Mac & Cheese

Ingredients

For the Mac & Cheese:

2 cups elbow macaroni

2 cups shredded Gouda cheese

1 cup whole milk

1/4 cup unsalted butter

Salt and black pepper to taste

For the Tagine Topping:

1 lb boneless chicken thighs, cut into bite-sized pieces

2 tablespoons olive oil

1 onion, finely chopped

1 teaspoon ground cumin

1 teaspoon ground coriander

1 teaspoon ground paprika

1/2 teaspoon ground cinnamon

2 cloves garlic, minced

1/2 teaspoon ground ginger

1/2 cup canned chickpeas, drained and rinsed

1/2 cup dried apricots, chopped

1/4 cup slivered almonds, toasted

Salt and black pepper to taste

Fresh cilantro leaves, for garnish

Lemon wedges, for serving

 **Prepare Time**
20 Minutes

 **Cook Time**
30 Minutes

We're taking a flavorful detour to Morocco on our Mac & Cheese World Adventure with a fusion that combines the exotic spices and aromas of Moroccan tagine with the creamy comfort of mac and cheese. Get ready for a tantalizing experience in our Moroccan Tagine Mac & Cheese!

Instructions

Step 1: Boil the Macaroni

Fill a large pot with water and add a pinch of salt.

Bring the water to a boil over high heat.

Add the elbow macaroni and cook according to the package instructions until they're "al dente" (usually about 7-8 minutes).

Drain the macaroni in a colander and set them aside.

Step 2: Prepare the Tagine Topping

In a large skillet or tagine (if available), heat the olive oil over medium-high heat.

Add the finely chopped onion and sauté for about 3-4 minutes until it becomes translucent.

Stir in the minced garlic and cook for an additional 1-2 minutes until fragrant.

Add the bite-sized chicken pieces and cook until they're browned on all sides, usually about 5-7 minutes.

Sprinkle in the ground cumin, ground coriander, ground paprika, ground cinnamon, and ground ginger. Stir well to coat the chicken with the aromatic spices.

Step 2: Prepare the Tagine Topping (Continued)

Add the canned chickpeas and chopped dried apricots to the skillet.

Season with salt and black pepper to taste.

Let the tagine mixture simmer for about 5-7 minutes to meld the flavors together.

Meanwhile, toast the slivered almonds in a dry skillet over medium heat until they're golden and fragrant.

Step 3: Make the Cheese Sauce

In a separate saucepan over medium heat, melt the butter. Once melted, add a pinch of salt and black pepper.

Pour in the whole milk and stir until it's heated through.

Reduce the heat to low and add the shredded Gouda cheese, stirring until the cheese is fully melted and the sauce is smooth.

Step 4: Combine Macaroni and Tagine

Add the cooked macaroni to the Gouda cheese sauce and stir until the macaroni is evenly coated with the creamy goodness.

Then, gently fold in the Moroccan tagine mixture, ensuring that the chicken, chickpeas, and apricots are evenly distributed throughout the mac and cheese.

Garnish and Serve

Garnish with toasted slivered almonds and fresh cilantro leaves.

Spoon your Moroccan Tagine Mac & Cheese into bowls.

Serve with lemon wedges on the side for a zesty touch.

 **Pro Tips:**

- You can use lamb or beef instead of chicken for a more traditional tagine flavor.
- For extra heat and depth of flavor, add a pinch of cayenne pepper or harissa to the tagine mixture.
- Try using whole wheat macaroni for added nuttiness and texture.

Enjoy! Your Moroccan Tagine Mac & Cheese is a delightful blend of creamy comfort and the exotic flavors of Morocco. The aromatic spices and sweet apricots make it an unforgettable dish.

Swiss Fondue Mac & Cheese

Ingredients

For the Mac & Cheese:

2 cups elbow macaroni

2 cups shredded Gruyère cheese

1 cup whole milk

1/4 cup unsalted butter

Salt and white pepper to taste

A pinch of nutmeg, for that Swiss touch

For the Fondue Topping:

1 1/2 cups shredded Emmental cheese

1 1/2 cups shredded Appenzeller cheese (or more Gruyère if unavailable)

1 clove garlic, halved

1 cup of heavy cream

Freshly ground black pepper, to taste

Fresh crusty bread, cubed for dipping

Gherkins, for serving (traditional Swiss accompaniment)

 **Prepare Time**
20 Minutes

 **Cook Time**
30 Minutes

Guten Tag, young chefs! Our Mac & Cheese World Adventure takes us to Switzerland, famous for its cheese, with a fusion that combines the gooey delight of Swiss fondue with the creamy comfort of mac and cheese. Get ready for a warm and cheesy experience in our Swiss Fondue Mac & Cheese!

Instructions

Step 1: Boil the Macaroni

Fill a large pot with water and add a pinch of salt.

Bring the water to a boil over high heat.

Add the elbow macaroni and cook according to the package instructions until they're "al dente" (usually about 7-8 minutes).

Drain the macaroni in a colander and set them aside.

Step 2: Prepare the Fondue Topping

Rub the inside of a fondue pot (or a heavy-bottomed saucepan) with the cut sides of the garlic clove. This will infuse the pot with a subtle garlic flavor.

Pour the heavy cream into the fondue pot and heat it over medium-low heat until it simmers.

Gradually add the shredded Emmental and Appenzeller cheeses, stirring continuously in a figure-eight motion until the cheese is fully melted and the mixture is smooth.

Season with freshly ground black pepper to taste.

Step 3: Make the Cheese Sauce

In a separate saucepan over medium heat, melt the butter.

Step 3: Make the Cheese Sauce (Continued)

Once melted, add a pinch of salt and a pinch of white pepper. Pour in the whole milk and stir until it's heated through.

Reduce the heat to low and add the shredded Gruyère cheese, stirring until the cheese is fully melted and the sauce is smooth.

Add a pinch of nutmeg, a classic Swiss seasoning.

Step 4: Combine Macaroni and Fondue

Add the cooked macaroni to the Gruyère cheese sauce and stir until the macaroni is evenly coated with the creamy goodness.

Serve & Enjoy

Your Swiss Fondue Mac & Cheese is ready to be enjoyed! Spoon it into bowls.

Fondue Time! Gather around the fondue pot filled with your cheese fondue mixture.

Pro Tips:

- If you don't have a fondue pot, you can keep the cheese fondue warm in a slow cooker or a ceramic dish over a low flame.
- Dip cubes of fresh crusty bread into the cheese fondue using long forks. Make sure to stir the cheese mixture occasionally to prevent it from getting too thick.
- Enjoy your Swiss Fondue Mac & Cheese with gherkins on the side, a traditional Swiss accompaniment.

En guete (enjoy your meal in Swiss German)! Your Swiss Fondue Mac & Cheese is a delightful blend of creamy comfort and the rich, savory flavors of Switzerland. It's a perfect dish for gatherings and celebrations. Dip that crusty bread and savor the cheesy goodness.

Asian Specialty Mac and Cheese

Ingredients

For the Mac & Cheese:

2 cups elbow macaroni

2 cups shredded white chedder cheese

1 cup whole milk

1/4 cup unsalted butter

Salt and white pepper to taste

For the Asian Flare:

1 cup cooked and shredded chicken (you can also use tofu or shrimp)

1 cup mixed stir-fried vegetables (broccoli, bell peppers, carrots, snap peas - whatever you like!)

2 cloves garlic, minced

1 tablespoon ginger, grated

2 tablespoons soy sauce

1 tablespoon sesame oil

1 tablespoon honey

1 teaspoon sriracha sauce (adjust for your spice preference)

Chopped green onions and sesame seeds for garnish

 **Prepare Time**
20 Minutes

 **Cook Time**
30 Minutes

Let's dive into the fusion world of flavors with our Asian-inspired Mac and Cheese. This dish combines the creamy richness of white cheddar with the bold and vibrant tastes of Asia. Get ready for a culinary adventure that will tickle your taste buds and satisfy your cravings.

Instructions

Step 1: Boil the Macaroni

Start by boiling a large pot of water and adding a pinch of salt.

Bring the water to a boil over high heat.

Once the water is boiling, add the elbow macaroni and cook according to the package instructions until they're "al dente" (usually about 7-8 minutes).

Drain the macaroni in a colander and set them aside.

Step 2: Stir-Fry Your Asian Flare

In a large skillet or wok, heat some oil over medium-high heat.

Add the minced garlic and grated ginger and stir for about 30 seconds until fragrant.

Toss in your mixed stir-fried vegetables and sauté for 2-3 minutes until they're tender-crisp.

Add the cooked and shredded chicken (or your choice of protein) and continue stir-frying until it's heated through.

Pour in the soy sauce, sesame oil, honey, and sriracha sauce. Stir well to coat everything evenly. Taste and adjust the seasoning to your preference.

Step 3: Make the Cheese Sauce

In a separate saucepan over medium heat, melt the butter. Once melted, add a pinch of salt and white pepper.

Pour in the whole milk and stir until it's heated through.

Reduce the heat to low and add the shredded white cheddar cheese, stirring until the cheese is fully melted and the sauce is smooth.

Step 4: Combine Macaroni and Asian Flare

Add the cooked macaroni to the white cheddar cheese sauce and stir until the macaroni is beautifully coated with that creamy goodness.

Now comes the exciting part! Combine your cheesy macaroni with the Asian-flavored stir-fry mixture. Give it all a good mix, ensuring every bite has a taste of both worlds.

Garnish and Serve

Garnish with chopped green onions and a sprinkle of sesame seeds for a delightful crunch and burst of freshness.

Scoop your Asian Mac and Cheese onto plates.

 **Pro Tips:**

- Add some crushed peanuts or cashews for extra crunch and flavor.
- If you're vegetarian, skip the chicken and use tofu or your favorite meat substitute.
- Adjust the level of sriracha sauce to suit your spice tolerance.

Enjoy your culinary journey! This Asian Mac and Cheese with White Cheddar is a harmonious blend of creamy comfort and the vibrant, savory flavors of Asia. Savor every bite, and let your taste buds dance with joy.

Bayou Jambalaya Mac & Cheese

Ingredients

For the Mac & Cheese:

2 cups elbow macaroni

2 cups shredded pepper jack cheese

1 cup whole milk

1/4 cup unsalted butter

Salt and black pepper to taste

For the Jambalaya Topping:

1 cup cooked andouille sausage, sliced

1 cup cooked chicken breast, diced

1 cup cooked shrimp, peeled and deveined

1 cup diced bell peppers (a mix of red, green, and yellow)

1/2 cup diced onion

2 cloves garlic, minced

1 cup diced tomatoes

1 tablespoon Cajun seasoning

1/2 teaspoon hot sauce (adjust to your spice preference)

Salt and black pepper to taste

Chopped fresh parsley, for garnish

Prepare Time
20 Minutes

Cook Time
30 Minutes

Our Mac & Cheese World Adventure is taking us to the heart of the American South, where we're blending the zesty flavors of jambalaya with the creamy comfort of mac and cheese. Get ready for some Louisiana soul in our Bayou Jambalaya Mac & Cheese!

Instructions

Step 1: Boil the Macaroni

Fill a large pot with water and add a pinch of salt.

Bring the water to a boil over high heat.

Add the elbow macaroni and cook according to the package instructions until they're "al dente" (usually about 7-8 minutes).

Drain the macaroni in a colander and set them aside.

Step 2: Prepare the Jambalaya Topping

In a large skillet, heat some oil over medium-high heat.

Stir in the minced garlic and cook for an additional 1-2 minutes until fragrant.

Add the diced bell peppers to the skillet and sauté for about 3-4 minutes until they begin to soften.

Toss in the diced tomatoes and cook for another 2-3 minutes until they release their juices.

Stir in the andouille sausage, diced chicken breast, and peeled and deveined shrimp.

Season with Cajun seasoning, hot sauce, salt, and black pepper to taste.

Let the jambalaya mixture simmer for about 5-7 minutes until the shrimp turn pink, the chicken is heated through, and the flavors meld together.

Step 3: Make the Cheese Sauce

In a separate saucepan over medium heat, melt the butter. Once melted, add a pinch of salt and black pepper.

Pour in the whole milk and stir until it's heated through.

Reduce the heat to low and add the shredded pepper jack cheese, stirring until the cheese is fully melted and the sauce is smooth.

Step 4: Combine Macaroni and Jambalaya

Add the cooked macaroni to the pepper jack cheese sauce and stir until the macaroni is evenly coated with the creamy goodness.

Serve & Enjoy

Spoon your Bayou Jambalaya Mac & Cheese into bowls. Top with the jambalaya mixture.

Garnish with chopped fresh parsley for a burst of color and flavor.

 Pro Tips:

- For an extra kick of flavor, use smoked andouille sausage.
- Feel free to add some diced okra or chopped scallions to your jambalaya topping for a true Louisiana touch.
- Serve with a wedge of cornbread for the ultimate Southern experience.

Laissez les bons temps rouler (let the good times roll)! Your Bayou Jambalaya Mac & Cheese is a fusion of creamy comfort and the vibrant, spicy flavors of the Louisiana bayou. The jambalaya topping takes it to a whole new level.

Irish Colcannon Mac & Cheese

Ingredients

For the Mac & Cheese:

2 cups elbow macaroni

2 cups shredded Irish cheddar cheese (or regular cheddar if unavailable)

1 cup whole milk

1/4 cup unsalted butter

Salt and black pepper to taste

For the Colcannon Topping:

2 cups mashed potatoes (prepared beforehand)

1 cup chopped kale or cabbage (cooked and drained)

1/2 cup diced leeks (cooked and drained)

2 cloves garlic, minced

2 tablespoons butter

Salt and black pepper to taste

Fresh parsley, chopped, for garnish

 **Prepare Time**
20 Minutes

 **Cook Time**
30 Minutes

Top of the morning to you, young chefs! Our Mac & Cheese World Adventure has brought us to the Emerald Isle, where we're blending the cozy flavors of Irish colcannon with the creamy comfort of mac and cheese. Get ready for a taste of Ireland in our Irish Colcannon Mac & Cheese!

Instructions

Step 1: Boil the Macaroni

Start by boiling a large pot of water and adding a pinch of salt.

Bring the water to a boil over high heat.

Once the water is boiling, add the elbow macaroni and cook according to the package instructions until they're "al dente" (usually about 7-8 minutes).

Drain the macaroni in a colander and set them aside.

Step 2: Prepare the Colcannon Topping

In a skillet or pan, melt the butter over medium heat.

Add the minced garlic and sauté for about 1-2 minutes until fragrant.

Stir in the chopped kale or cabbage and diced leeks.

Cook for about 3-4 minutes until the greens are tender. Season with salt and black pepper to taste.

In a large mixing bowl, combine the cooked mashed potatoes and the sautéed greens mixture. Mix well to create your colcannon topping.

Step 3: Make the Cheese Sauce

In a separate saucepan over medium heat, melt the butter. Once melted, add a pinch of salt and black pepper.

Pour in the whole milk and stir until it's heated through.

Reduce the heat to low and add the shredded Irish cheddar cheese (or regular cheddar), stirring until the cheese is fully melted and the sauce is smooth.

Step 4: Combine Macaroni and Colcannon

Add the cooked macaroni to the cheddar cheese sauce and stir until the macaroni is evenly coated with the creamy goodness.

Garnish and Serve

Spoon your Irish Colcannon Mac & Cheese into bowls. Top with generous dollops of the colcannon mixture.

Garnish with chopped fresh parsley for a pop of color and flavor.

Pro Tips:

- Irish cheddar cheese has a distinct sharp flavor, but you can substitute with regular cheddar if needed.
- use other leafy greens like spinach or Swiss chard if you prefer.
- Serve with a side of Irish soda bread for an authentic Irish meal.

Sláinte (cheers), young chefs! Your Irish Colcannon Mac & Cheese is a delightful fusion of creamy comfort and the hearty flavors of the Irish countryside. The colcannon topping adds a unique twist to this classic dish.

Turkish Börek Mac & Cheese

Ingredients

For the Mac & Cheese:

2 cups elbow macaroni

2 cups shredded feta cheese

1 cup whole milk

1/4 cup unsalted butter

Salt and black pepper to taste

For the Börek Topping:

10 sheets of phyllo dough, thawed

1 cup chopped spinach (cooked and drained)

1/2 cup crumbled Turkish beyaz peynir (white cheese, or substitute with feta)

2 tablespoons chopped fresh parsley

2 cloves garlic, minced

Salt and black pepper to taste

Sesame seeds, for garnish (optional)

✓ **Prepare Time**
   20 Minutes

✓ **Cook Time**
   30 Minutes

Merhaba, young chefs! Our Mac & Cheese World Adventure takes a delightful detour to Turkey, where we're combining the flaky deliciousness of börek with the creamy comfort of mac and cheese. Get ready for a taste of the Mediterranean in our Turkish Börek Mac & Cheese!

Instructions

Step 1: Boil the Macaroni

Fill a large pot with water and add a pinch of salt.

Bring the water to a boil over high heat.

Add the elbow macaroni and cook according to the package instructions until they're "al dente" (usually about 7-8 minutes).

Drain the macaroni in a colander and set them aside.

Step 2: Prepare the Börek Topping

In a skillet, melt the butter over low heat.

Stir in the minced garlic and cook for about 1-2 minutes until fragrant.

Add the chopped spinach to the skillet and cook for 3-4 minutes until it's heated through and any excess moisture has evaporated.

In a mixing bowl, combine the cooked spinach, crumbled beyaz peynir (or feta), chopped fresh parsley, salt, and black pepper. Mix well to create your börek filling.

Step 3: Layer the Phyllo Dough

Preheat your oven to 350°F (180°C).

Take one sheet of phyllo dough and brush it generously with melted butter.

Place another sheet on top and repeat the process until you have 5 layers.

Spread the börek filling evenly over the top layer of phyllo.

Step 4: Roll and Bake

Carefully roll up the layered phyllo dough from one end to the other, creating a log. Place the börek log in a baking dish.

Brush the top with more melted butter and sprinkle with sesame seeds if desired.

Bake in the preheated oven for about 25-30 minutes or until the börek is golden brown and crispy.

Step 5: Make the Cheese Sauce

In a separate saucepan over medium heat, melt the butter. Once melted, add a pinch of salt and black pepper.

Pour in the whole milk and stir until it's heated through.

Reduce the heat to low and add the shredded feta cheese, stirring until the cheese is fully melted and the sauce is smooth.

Step 6: Combine Macaroni and Börek

Add the cooked macaroni to the feta cheese sauce and stir until the macaroni is evenly coated with the creamy goodness.

Garnish and Serve

Spoon your Turkish Börek Mac & Cheese into bowls.

Slice the baked börek log into rounds and place a round on top of each serving. Garnish with additional fresh parsley if desired.

Pro Tips:

- Be gentle when working with phyllo dough, as it can tear easily. Keep a damp kitchen towel on top of the sheets you're not using to prevent them from drying out.
- Adjust the level of garlic and spices to your preference for the börek filling.
- Serve with a dollop of yogurt or a squeeze of lemon for an extra burst of flavor.

Afiyet olsun (enjoy your meal)! Your Turkish Börek Mac & Cheese is a delicious fusion of creamy comfort and the savory flavors of Turkey. The crispy börek topping adds a delightful crunch.

Cuban Ropa Vieja Mac & Cheese

Ingredients

For the Mac & Cheese:

2 cups elbow macaroni

2 cups shredded Monterey Jack cheese

1 cup whole milk

1/4 cup unsalted butter

Salt and black pepper to taste

For the Ropa Vieja Topping:

1 lb flank steak 1 onion, finely chopped

1 red bell pepper, thinly sliced

1 green bell pepper, thinly sliced

2 cloves garlic, minced

1 can (14 oz) crushed tomatoes

1 teaspoon ground cumin

1 teaspoon paprika

1/2 teaspoon dried oregano

Salt and black pepper to taste

Olive oil, for cooking

Sliced green olives and fresh cilantro, for garnish

Lime wedges, for serving

 **Prepare Time**
20 Minutes

 **Cook Time**
30 Minutes

¡Hola, young chefs! Our Mac & Cheese World Adventure has brought us to the lively streets of Cuba, where we're combining the hearty flavors of Ropa Vieja with the creamy comfort of mac and cheese. Get ready to dance to the rhythms of Havana in our Cuban Ropa Vieja Mac & Cheese!

Instructions

Step 1: Boil the Macaroni

Start by boiling a large pot of water and adding a pinch of salt.

Bring the water to a boil over high heat.

Once the water is boiling, add the elbow macaroni and cook according to the package instructions until they're "al dente" (usually about 7-8 minutes).

Drain the macaroni in a colander and set them aside.

Step 2: Prepare the Ropa Vieja Topping

Season the flank steak generously with salt and black pepper. In a skillet or pan, heat some olive oil over medium-high heat.

Add the seasoned flank steak and sear it on both sides until it's browned (about 3-4 minutes per side).

Remove the steak from the skillet and let it rest for a few minutes.

In the same skillet, add a bit more olive oil if needed.

Stir in the finely chopped onion and thinly sliced red and green bell peppers. Sauté for about 5-7 minutes until the vegetables become tender.

Add the minced garlic and cook for an additional 1-2 minutes until fragrant.

Step 2: Prepare the Ropa Vieja Topping (Continued)

Return the seared flank steak to the skillet and pour in the crushed tomatoes.

Season with ground cumin, paprika, dried oregano, salt, and black pepper.

Cover the skillet, reduce the heat to low, and let the mixture simmer for about 1.5 to 2 hours until the steak is tender and easily shreds.

Shred the cooked flank steak using two forks and stir it into the flavorful tomato and pepper mixture.

Step 3: Make the Cheese Sauce

In a separate saucepan over medium heat, melt the butter. Once melted, add a pinch of salt and black pepper.

Pour in the whole milk and stir until it's heated through.

Reduce the heat to low and add the shredded Monterey Jack cheese, stirring until the cheese is fully melted and the sauce is smooth.

Step 4: Combine Macaroni and Ropa Vieja

Add the cooked macaroni to the Monterey Jack cheese sauce and stir until the macaroni is evenly coated with the creamy goodness.

Garnish and Serve

Spoon your Cuban Ropa Vieja Mac & Cheese into bowls.

Top with generous scoops of the Ropa Vieja mixture.

 Pro Tips:

- You can also use shredded beef brisket or roast pork as a tasty alternative to flank steak.
- Serve with a side of black beans and rice for a complete Cuban meal. Adjust the level of spice with a dash of hot sauce if you like it fiery.
- Garnish with sliced green olives, fresh cilantro, and lime wedges for squeezing over the top.

¡Buen provecho (enjoy your meal), young chefs! Your Cuban Ropa Vieja Mac & Cheese is a fusion of creamy comfort and the rich, savory flavors of Cuba. The Ropa Vieja topping adds a unique and hearty twist to this classic dish.

Filipino Adobo Mac & Cheese

Ingredients

For the Mac & Cheese:

2 cups elbow macaroni

2 cups shredded sharp cheddar cheese

1 cup whole milk

1/4 cup unsalted butter

Salt and black pepper to taste

For the Adobo Topping:

1 lb boneless chicken thighs (you can also use pork or a combination of both)

1 onion, finely chopped

4 cloves garlic, minced

1/2 cup soy sauce

1/2 cup white vinegar

1 bay leaf

1 teaspoon whole black peppercorns

1/2 teaspoon dried oregano

1/2 teaspoon brown sugar

Salt and black pepper to taste

Cooking oil, for searing the meat

Fresh cilantro and sliced green onions, for garnish

Prepare Time
20 Minutes

Cook Time
30 Minutes

Kamusta, young chefs! Our Mac & Cheese World Adventure takes us to the beautiful Philippines, where we're blending the savory flavors of Adobo with the creamy comfort of mac and cheese. Get ready for a mouthwatering fusion of flavors.

Instructions

Step 1: Boil the Macaroni

Fill a large pot with water and add a pinch of salt.

Bring the water to a boil over high heat.

Once the water is boiling, add the elbow macaroni and cook according to the package instructions until they're "al dente" (usually about 7-8 minutes).

Drain the macaroni in a colander and set them aside.

Step 2: Prepare the Adobo Topping

Cut the boneless chicken thighs into bite-sized pieces.

In a large skillet or pan, heat some cooking oil over medium- high heat.

Add the chopped onion and minced garlic, sautéing for about 3- 4 minutes until they become fragrant and translucent.

Stir in the chicken (or pork) pieces and cook until they are browned on all sides.

Pour in the soy sauce, white vinegar, and add the bay leaf, whole black peppercorns, dried oregano, brown sugar, salt, and black pepper.

Stir to combine and bring the mixture to a simmer.

Step 2: Prepare the Adobo Topping (Continued)

Cover the skillet, reduce the heat to low, and let it simmer for about 25-30 minutes until the meat is tender, and the sauce has thickened.

Remove the bay leaf before serving.

Step 3: Make the Cheese Sauce

In a separate saucepan over medium heat, melt the butter. Once melted, add a pinch of salt and black pepper.

Pour in the whole milk and stir until it's heated through.

Reduce the heat to low and add the shredded sharp cheddar cheese, stirring until the cheese is fully melted and the sauce is smooth.

Step 4: Combine Macaroni and Adobo

Add the cooked macaroni to the sharp cheddar cheese sauce and stir until the macaroni is evenly coated with the creamy goodness.

Garnish and Serve

Spoon your Filipino Adobo Mac & Cheese into bowls.

Top with generous scoops of the Adobo mixture.

Garnish with fresh cilantro and sliced green onions.

 **Pro Tips:**

- Adjust the balance of vinegar and soy sauce to suit your taste.
- Add a bit of chili pepper for a spicy kick.

Magandang kainan (enjoy your meal)! Your Filipino Adobo Mac & Cheese is a fusion of creamy comfort and the bold, savory flavors of the Philippines. The Adobo topping adds a delightful twist to this classic dish.

German Sausage Mac & Cheese

Ingredients

For the Mac & Cheese:

2 cups elbow macaroni

2 cups shredded Emmental cheese (or Gouda if unavailable)

1 cup whole milk

1/4 cup unsalted butter

Salt and white pepper to taste

For the Sausage Topping:

4 German sausages (Bratwurst or Weisswurst)

1 onion, finely chopped

2 cloves garlic, minced

1 tablespoon olive oil

1 teaspoon caraway seeds (optional)

1/4 cup German mustard

1/4 cup sauerkraut, drained

Fresh parsley, chopped, for garnish

Prepare Time
20 Minutes

Cook Time
30 Minutes

Our Mac & Cheese World Adventure is taking us to the heart of Europe, where we're blending the savory flavors of German sausages with the creamy comfort of mac and cheese. Get ready to savor the flavors of Deutschland in our German Sausage Mac & Cheese!

Instructions

Step 1: Boil the Macaroni

Start by boiling a large pot of water and adding a pinch of salt.

Once the water is boiling, add the elbow macaroni and cook according to the package instructions until they're "al dente" (usually about 7-8 minutes).

Drain the macaroni in a colander and set them aside.

Step 2: Prepare the Sausage Topping

In a skillet or pan, heat the olive oil over medium-high heat.

Add the finely chopped onion and sauté for about 3-4 minutes until they become translucent.

Stir in the minced garlic and caraway seeds (if using), cooking for an additional 1-2 minutes until fragrant.

Add the German sausages to the skillet and cook them until they're browned on all sides, about 5-7 minutes.

Remove the sausages from the skillet and slice them into rounds.

In the same skillet, add the sauerkraut and cook for a few minutes until it's heated through.

Step 3: Make the Cheese Sauce

In a separate saucepan over medium heat, melt the butter. Once melted, add a pinch of salt and white pepper.

Pour in the whole milk and stir until it's heated through.

Reduce the heat to low and add the shredded Emmental cheese (or Gouda), stirring until the cheese is fully melted and the sauce is smooth.

Step 4: Combine Macaroni and Sausage

Add the cooked macaroni to the cheese sauce and stir until the macaroni is evenly coated with the creamy goodness.

Garnish and Serve

Spoon your German Sausage Mac & Cheese into bowls.

Top with generous scoops of the sliced sausage and sauerkraut mixture.

Drizzle with German mustard and garnish with fresh chopped parsley.

 Pro Tips:

- Serve with a side of warm pretzels for an authentic German touch.
- If you can't find Emmental cheese, Gouda or Swiss cheese works well too.
- Add a dollop of sour cream for extra creaminess.

Guten Appetit (enjoy your meal)! Your German Sausage Mac & Cheese is a fusion of creamy comfort and the rich, savory flavors of Germany. The sausage topping adds a delightful and hearty twist to this classic dish.

Swedish Meatball Mac & Cheese

Ingredients

For the Mac & Cheese:

2 cups elbow macaroni

2 cups shredded Swedish Västerbotten cheese (or sharp cheddar if unavailable)

1 cup whole milk

1/4 cup unsalted butter

Salt and white pepper to taste

For the Swedish Meatballs:

1 lb ground beef (or a mixture of beef and pork)

1/2 cup breadcrumbs

1/4 cup whole milk

1/2 onion, finely chopped

1 clove garlic, minced

1/4 teaspoon ground allspice

1/4 teaspoon ground nutmeg

Salt and black pepper to taste

Butter or cooking oil, for frying

For the Creamy Gravy:

2 cups beef or vegetable broth

1/4 cup heavy cream

2 tablespoons all-purpose flour

Salt and black pepper, to taste

Prepare Time
20 Minutes

Cook Time
30 Minutes

Hej, young chefs! Our Mac & Cheese World Adventure now takes us to the charming country of Sweden, where we'll blend the savory flavors of Swedish meatballs with the creamy comfort of mac and cheese. Get ready for a delightful fusion in our Swedish Meatball Mac & Cheese!

Instructions

Step 1: Boil the Macaroni

Fill a large pot with water and add a pinch of salt.

Bring the water to a boil over high heat.

Add the elbow macaroni and cook according to the package instructions until they're "al dente" (usually about 7-8 minutes).

Drain the macaroni in a colander and set them aside.

Step 2: Prepare the Swedish Meatballs

In a bowl, combine the breadcrumbs and whole milk. Let them soak for a few minutes.

In a separate bowl, mix the ground beef (or beef and pork mixture), finely chopped onion, minced garlic, ground allspice, ground nutmeg, salt, and black pepper.

Add the breadcrumb mixture to the meat mixture and mix until everything is well combined.

Shape the mixture into small meatballs, about 1 inch in diameter.

In a large skillet or pan, heat some butter or cooking oil over medium-high heat.

Step 2: Prepare the Swedish Meatballs (Continued)

Add the meatballs and cook until they're browned on all sides and cooked through, about 5-7 minutes.

Remove the meatballs from the skillet and set them aside.

Step 3: Make the Creamy Gravy

In the same skillet you used for the meatballs, add the all-purpose flour.

Cook the flour over medium heat for about 1-2 minutes until it's lightly browned. Gradually whisk in the beef or vegetable broth and heavy cream.

Continue to whisk until the mixture thickens and becomes a smooth gravy. Season with salt and black pepper to taste.

Add the cooked meatballs back into the skillet and let them simmer in the creamy gravy for a few minutes.

Step 4: Make the Cheese Sauce

In a separate saucepan over medium heat, melt the butter. Once melted, add a pinch of salt and white pepper.

Pour in the whole milk and stir until it's heated through.

Reduce the heat to low and add the shredded Swedish Västerbotten cheese (or sharp cheddar), stirring until the cheese is fully melted and the sauce is smooth.

Step 5: Combine Macaroni, Meatballs, and Cheese

Add the cooked macaroni to the cheese sauce and stir until the macaroni is evenly coated with the creamy goodness.

Garnish and Serve

Spoon your Swedish Meatball Mac & Cheese into bowls. Top with the creamy Swedish meatballs and gravy.

 Pro Tips:

- Serve your Swedish Meatball Mac & Cheese with lingonberry sauce or cranberry sauce for a sweet and tart contrast.
- Add a sprinkle of fresh chopped parsley for a burst of color and freshness.
- For a vegetarian twist, replace the meatballs with Swedish-style veggie meatballs.

Smaklig måltid (enjoy your meal)! Your Swedish Meatball Mac & Cheese is a fusion of creamy comfort and the rich, savory flavors of Sweden. The Swedish meatball topping adds a delightful and heartwarming twist to this classic dish.

Hawaiian Huli Huli Mac & Cheese

Ingredients

For the Mac & Cheese:

2 cups elbow macaroni

2 cups shredded Monterey Jack cheese

1 cup whole milk

1/4 cup unsalted butter

Salt and white pepper to taste

For the Huli Huli Chicken Topping:

1 lb boneless chicken thighs, skinless

1/2 cup pineapple juice

1/4 cup soy sauce

1/4 cup ketchup

1/4 cup brown sugar

2 tablespoons rice vinegar

1 tablespoon grated fresh ginger

2 cloves garlic, minced

Pineapple rings (canned or fresh) for garnish

Chopped fresh cilantro for garnish

 **Prepare Time**
20 Minutes

Cook Time
30 Minutes

Aloha, adventurous cooks! We're about to embark on a tropical journey that fuses the creamy delight of mac and cheese with the sweet and savory flavors of Hawaii's famous Huli Huli chicken. Get ready for a Hawaiian Luau in your kitchen with our Hawaiian Huli Huli Mac & Cheese!

Instructions

Step 1: Boil the Macaroni

Start by boiling a large pot of water and adding a pinch of salt.

Bring the water to a boil over high heat.

Once the water is boiling, add the elbow macaroni and cook according to the package instructions until they're "al dente" (usually about 7-8 minutes).

Drain the macaroni in a colander and set them aside.

Step 2: Prepare the Huli Huli Chicken

In a bowl, whisk together the pineapple juice, soy sauce, ketchup, brown sugar, rice vinegar, grated ginger, and minced garlic. This is your Huli Huli sauce.

Place the boneless chicken thighs in a resealable plastic bag or shallow dish and pour half of the Huli Huli sauce over them. Seal the bag or cover the dish and marinate in the fridge for at least 20 minutes.

Step 3: Cook the Chicken

Preheat your grill or a grill pan over medium-high heat.

Remove the chicken thighs from the marinade and grill them for about 4-5 minutes per side, or until they're cooked through and have those beautiful grill marks.

Step 3: Cook the Chicken (Continued)

While grilling, brush the chicken with the remaining Huli Huli sauce to get that sweet and savory glaze.

Once done, remove the chicken from the grill and let them rest for a few minutes. Then, slice them into thin strips.

Step 4: Make the Cheese Sauce

In a separate saucepan over medium heat, melt the butter.

Once it's all melty, add a pinch of salt and white pepper.

Pour in the whole milk and give it a good stir until it's warmed up.

Reduce the heat to low and add the shredded Monterey Jack cheese, stirring until it's fully melted and the sauce is luxuriously smooth.

Step 5: Combine Macaroni, Chicken, and Cheese

Mix the cooked macaroni into your creamy cheese sauce, making sure every noodle gets a cozy cheese bath.

Step 6: Bring It All Together

Here comes the fun part! Combine your cheesy macaroni with those mouthwatering strips of Huli Huli chicken. Give it all a good stir, so every bite gets a taste of both worlds.

Garnish and Serve

Plate up your Hawaiian Huli Huli Mac & Cheese.

Garnish with pineapple rings and a sprinkle of chopped fresh cilantro for that extra island flair.

 **Pro Tips:**

- Want to add some extra tropical vibes? Grill some pineapple rings and serve them alongside.
- Sprinkle chopped Macadamia nuts to add more Ono local taste.
- Adjust the sweetness of the Huli Huli sauce by adding more or less brown sugar to suit your taste.

Mahalo (thank you), Young Chef adventurer! Your Hawaiian Huli Huli Mac & Cheese is a perfect blend of creamy comfort and the sweet, savory flavors of Hawaii. Every bite will transport you to the beautiful shores of the Aloha State.

Lil Chef Notes

Print out the next page "Lil Chef Notes" and use to keep track of any modifications you do to a recipe. Or you can simply keep any type of notes you want for any of the recipes so you can reference again later. For instance ingredient substitutions or a maybe you used less or more of recommended measurement for taste preferences.

Lil Chef Notes

RECIPE NAME:

_____
_____
_____
_____
_____
_____
_____
_____
_____
_____

ADD/REMOVE INGREDIENTS & MEASURES:
- ☐ _____
- ☐ _____
- ☐ _____
- ☐ _____
- ☐ _____

SUBSTITUTE INGREDIENTS AND MEASURES:
- ☐ _____
- ☐ _____
- ☐ _____
- ☐ _____
- ☐ _____

Your feedback is greatly appreciated!

It's through your feedback, support and reviews that I'm able to create the best books possible and serve more people.

I would be extremely grateful if you could take just 60 seconds to kindly leave an honest review of the book on Amazon. Please share your feedback and thoughts for others to see.

To do so, simply find the book on Amazon's website (or where you purchased my book from) and locate the section to leave a review.

Select a star rating and don't forget to let us know what your favorite recipes are :)

Write a customer review

Follow us on Instagram: letsgochefkc
Share your cooking photos and videos. We'd love to see those yummy dishes!

Have a question or want to share your experience and photos? **Email:** chefkc@chefsletsgo.com